# We Have A Problem

## LET'S SOLVE IT!

RIMMA MELLO

**ISBN-13: 978-0996054911**
**ISBN-10: 099605491X**

Cover design and all artwork created by

**Mikal Harris**

For *Animation Rules*; a subsidiary of **W.O.M.B. Publications**

©Copyright 2014 W.O.M.B. Publications, Jersey City, NJ

# We Have A Problem
## LET'S SOLVE IT!

RIMMA MELLO

"This book is dedicated to the children and staff at Play and Learn School".


-Rimma Mello

"Hi I'm Sara"

"and I'm Ashley."

We have a problem.

Let's solve it.

Sara: "I want the orange dress!"

Ashley: "I want the orange dress! Uh-oh We both want the orange dress!"

Sara and Ashley are upset. They both want the orange dress. Let's solve the problem.

"We will take turns", says Sara.
They will use the clock to time the turns.

5 minutes

Sara: "I am waiting!"

Ashley: "I am playing. Soon I will give it to you!"

Time is up for Ashley. Now it's Sara's turn to play with the dress.

Ashley gives Sara the dress.

Sara: "Thank you!"

Ashley: "This is the way we solved the problem!"

We had fun solving
the problem.

Sara: Bye!

Ashley: Bye!

The
End!

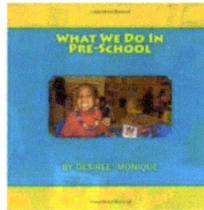

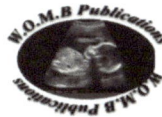